Collection of teddy bears and a plush penguin awaiting sale at a London auction house.

TEDDY BEARS AND SOFT TOYS

Pauline Cockrill

Shire Publications Ltd

CONTENTS

Published in 1997 by Shire Publications Ltd, Cromwell House, Church Street, Princes Risborough, Buckinghamshire HP27 9AA, UK.

Printed in Great Britain by CIT Printing Services, Press Buildings, Merlins Bridge, Haverfordwest, Pembrokeshire SA61 1XF.

British Library Cataloguing in Publication Data: Cockrill, Pauline. *Teddy Bears and Soft Toys*. 1. Soft Toys. Making. – Manuals. I. Title. 745.592'4. ISBN 0-85263-968-6.

Cover: *(From left) Teddy bear in sailor suit, probably English, about 1911; small teddy bear (sitting), German by Steiff, about 1920; blonde teddy bear, standing, German by Steiff, about 1910; teddy bear in pyjamas, English by Merrythought, about 1935; (front) Mickey Mouse, English, Dean's Rag Book Company, about 1930.*

Below: *Early German teddy bear of about 1905, made by Steiff, with photographs of the original owners.*

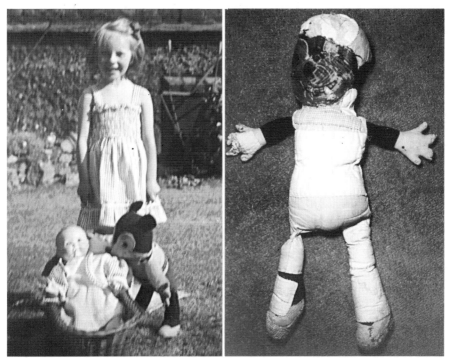

Mickey Mouse soft toy in mint condition (left) with its first owner in about 1951 and (right) virtually unrecognisable after several years of use.

INTRODUCTION

Today the term soft toy is understood to mean a plaything made from woven or knitted cloth or animal skin. The very nature of these materials makes soft toys highly desirable and they afford security to many infants. Most commonly, soft toys are rag dolls or cuddly fabric animals and are often a child's first possession.

The role of the soft toy as a much hugged comforter, combined with the inherent fragility and fugitive quality of fur and textiles, has meant that, even where toys have survived the clutches of a child and have found their way into the hands of a collector, they are often extremely worn and sometimes virtually unrecognisable. Within our own experience, we are probably aware of a favourite soft toy which barely resembles its pristine state.

We must assume that such toys were being made from earliest times, simple dolls and animals being fashioned by a parent or child from scraps of readily available material. There is, for instance, a small, coarsely woven rag doll in the British Museum, which was excavated from a child's tomb in Oxyrhynchus, Egypt. This rare example dates from the Roman occupation of about 300 BC.

However, the majority of soft toys found today in museums and private collections date from the late nineteenth century, a period which saw the beginning of their production on a widespread, commercial scale. On the other hand, it is possible that the manufacture of the mass-produced soft toy may have occurred prior to that date. For example, it has been suggested that the small

3

wheeled horse with its ruched linen coat (to be seen in the scullery of Ann Sharp's Baby House of about 1700), may have been commercially produced. However, with few early soft toys in existence, research in this area is limited. Even pictorial evidence cannot reliably give details of the materials used in a toy animal's or doll's manufacture.

This book surveys the development of the manufactured soft toy readily available from the 1880s to the years immediately following the Second World War, using both the surviving toys themselves as well as the contents of trade catalogues as examples. Special attention is paid to the teddy bear, whose creation has to be seen as the single most significant boost for the embryonic soft toy industry in the early years of the twentieth century. Certainly, the teddy bear has enjoyed continual success in the nursery, outliving many rivals, from the ill-fated 'Billy Possum' of 1909 to the numerous cloth novelty toys produced during the interwar period. From the late 1970s, the teddy also became an increasingly popular item in the saleroom and the burgeoning interest in its serious collection has led to the formation of a new word, 'arctophily', to describe this hobby (from the Greek: *arktos*, bear; *philos*, love).

Above: *A rare survivor: a rag doll found in a Roman grave in Egypt, dating from about 300 BC; 7 inches (178 mm) long.*

"Eyes Right."
The Latest Soft Toy.
12/- 20/- 28/- 40/- 60/-
84/- per doz.

Left: *This unidentified plush Highland bear/ dog appeared in an advertisement for Hamleys in 'Games and Toys' of the First World War period. It was made by Harwin and Company of London as a patriotic mascot. In the Museum of Childhood, Edinburgh.*

4

Left: *Steiff rabbit, about 1911, alongside what is possibly the rare 'Billy Possum', about 1909, mascot of the United States President elect, William Taft, and thus rival to Roosevelt's 'Teddy Bear'.*

Right: *Steiff monkey of plush and felt with glass eyes and stuffed with wood-wool, about 1910. In the Bethnal Green Museum of Childhood.*

STUFFED ANIMALS

We know that some of the first soft toy animals made commercially, in the late nineteenth century, were of rabbit skins. This, however, would have been expensive, especially if practised on a large scale, so a substitute fur fabric was developed in Britain. Woven mainly in Huddersfield and Dewsbury, it was known as Yorkshire Cloth. In the United States it is sometimes referred to as mohair plush or Teddy Bear Cloth. This pile fabric, commonly a mixture of mohair, wool and cotton, was originally exported from Britain to Germany, for it was the Germans who monopolised the manufacture of stuffed animal toys and almost all other spheres of the toy industry until the First World War.

The most important figure in the early history of the manufacture of soft toy animals is that of Margarete Steiff (1847-1909); her significance is further explained in the section on teddy bears. Crippled by polio as a child, she earned her living as a seamstress making ladies' and children's clothes in her home town of Giengen an der Brenz in southern Germany. In 1880 she made a felt pincushion in the shape of an elephant, which she later adapted into a toy for her young nephews and nieces. From this, she had the idea of making other felt animals and by 1900 she was engaged in a small family business manufacturing soft toys. Following the success of the teddy bear, a new factory was built in 1903 and here a wide variety of plush animals was made and distributed all over the world. Among the many soft toys made by German firms in the period before the First World War, those by Steiff are the easiest to identify: all

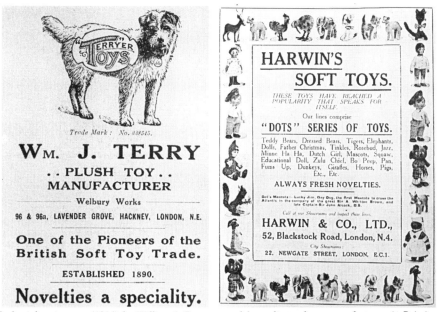

Left: *Advertisement (1916) for William J. Terry, one of the earliest soft toy manufacturers in Britain.*

Right: *Advertisement for Harwin and Company, founded in 1914 following the general ban on German imports. It was they who manufactured the two mascots which crossed the Atlantic with Alcock and Brown in 1919.*

Steiff's products were (and still are) marked with a small metal button in the left ear.

Although a pre-1914 plush toy animal is very likely to be German in origin, there were also a handful of British soft toy firms in operation at this time. The earliest of these London-based manufacturers was William J. Terry of Hackney, who produced his 'Terry'er Toys' from 1890 to the mid 1920s. Nearby in Stoke Newington, the British United Toy Manufacturing Company (formed in 1894) made numerous plush animals under the name of 'Omega' until the early 1980s. Coincidentally, another rival firm, J. K. Farnell of Acton and, later, Hastings (1897-1968), had the trademark 'Alpha Toys'.

Several new British soft toy firms were established during the First World War and flourished owing to the general ban on German imports. Many of these businesses reflected German ideas. W. H. Jones, for example, had been a toy manufacturer's agent prior to the war, and therefore knew German toys well. In 1914 he set up his soft toy business in a back room in the City of London with six seamstresses. By the end of the war he had moved to a larger factory nearby and had opened another in Penge.

Since few soft toys have survived, we need to look at trade catalogues to discover the kinds of animals produced at this time. Domestic animals (cats, dogs, rabbits, ducks) seem to have been most favoured, such as Dean's plush 'Kuddle-mee' series of about 1915. However, following Steiff's example, elephants and monkeys were also popular. Wood-wool, that is, fine-quality wood shavings, sometimes known as straw stuffing or excelsior, was generally used as a filling. Kapok, a natural silky fibre from the seeds of the Indonesian-grown kapok tree, was used more frequently by the 1920s, being lighter and more hygienic.

The 1920s and 1930s saw various changes in the manufacture of soft toy

Left: *Advertisement for the British United Toy Manufacturing Company, 1920s. Their founder, James Renvoize, introduced rayon or artificial silk plush to the soft toy industry.*

Right: *Soft toy black cats were popular mascots in the 1920s and 1930s. Some were German, like this 'Schuco' example, but they were also made in Britain. In the Bethnal Green Museum of Childhood.*

animals. Firstly, several new firms were established in Britain, including: the soft toy division of the old Birmingham-based toy firm of Chad Valley (1920); H. G. Stone (also 1920); Merrythought of Ironbridge, Shropshire (1930); and Pedigree, part of the Lines Bros Group in Merton (1937). These manufacturers, together with Dean's and Farnell, led the market in Britain. Secondly, the variety of animals was seen to increase. Particularly popular at this time were the many types of dog which were produced by nearly every company. Unless they possess a maker's label, it is very difficult today to determine their point of origin. Merrythought, for example, produced twenty different breeds within their first three years. Even quite obscure breeds were manufactured, such as H. G. Stone's Borzois (Russian Wolfhounds) as part of their 1928 'Panurge Pets' on wheels range.

New materials were introduced, such as artificial silk or rayon plush (made from reconstituted wood-pulp), and velveteen, a cheaper cotton-based form of velvet. The latter was used particularly for the many caricatured animals which became all the rage during the inter-war period. For example, H. G. Stone's 'Pêche Melba', a comical dog of 1926, was described as a 'confection in velvet'.

Steiff's trademark, a pewter-coloured button, with raised lettering. This style was used by the firm from 1905 to about 1950; 3/16 inch (5 mm) in diameter.

Velveteen bulldog mascot, made by Chad Valley in about 1930. Woven label: 'HYGIENIC TOYS. MADE IN ENGLAND BY CHAD VALLEY CO. LTD.' After 1938, a printed label was used: 'BY ROYAL APPOINTMENT TO H.M. QUEEN ELIZABETH.' In Bethnal Green Museum of Childhood.

Dean's, in particular, concentrated on caricatured animals and produced several in the mid 1920s. Most famous is perhaps 'Dismal Desmond', a printed cotton dalmatian. There was also 'Galloping Gus', a novel caricature of an old 'bus horse', and 'Thirsty', a dog whose tongue could change from red to blue according to the weather. Several toys were produced for charity purposes, for example, 'Tatters the Hospital Pup' and his son, 'Patient Pat'.

Toy pandas became popular following the arrival of 'Ming', the first giant panda at London Zoo, in 1938. Several firms made pandas from that date, including Merrythought, which was requested by the zoo to make a 'stand-in' baby panda for use during filming sessions. Many other animal toys were produced in response to events at London Zoo, such as the litter of lion cubs born in 1923, the birth of Jubilee the chimpanzee in 1935 and the polar bear cubs, Brumas (1949) and Pipaluk (1968).

The Second World War had a dramatic effect on the whole toy industry. Yorkshire Cloth was no longer made, as textile mills turned to essential war work. Toys were scarce and children had to depend on their own or their parents' skills with needle and thread. Soft toys were therefore largely made in the home or by women's groups from scraps of lambswool and cloth, or were knitted following the many patterns that were published at this period. As wool was rationed, it was common for old garments to be unravelled and reused.

The post-war period saw the introduction of man-made fabrics, such as nylon and polyester, which were used for both the plush and the stuffing of soft toys. Closer attention was paid to hygiene and safety, owing to new laws regarding soft toys passed at this time. Glass eyes, for example, were replaced by plastic ones and made safer by a locking system introduced in 1948 by Wendy Boston Playsafe Toys.

Several of the well established British soft toy firms went out of business in the 1960s and 1970s, unable to compete with the cheaper products made in the Far East, often on behalf of American firms, such as R. Dakin and Company.

8

Right: *Dean's Rag Book Company's 'Dismal Desmond' of 1926. He was also produced on all fours, with long back legs and in a smaller size in velveteen. A 'Cheerful Desmond' was later produced. In the Bethnal Green Museum of Childhood.*

Below: *'Jacko the Monkey' was made during the 1940s, when toys were scarce, from the accompanying pattern, 'Leach's Knitted Toys', printed by Newnes and Pearson Printing Company Limited. In the Bethnal Green Museum of Childhood.*

Above left: *In the twentieth century the teddy bear is very often one of our earliest possessions. Photograph about 1920.*

Above right: *Early Steiff teddy bear, about 1905. The humped back, black boot-button eyes, large feet and long curved paws are particularly typical of the maker and period.*

Right: *Steiff teddy bear. Around the time of the First World War glass eyes replaced the black buttons used previously.*

10

British teddy bear factory, as illustrated in Arthur Mee's 'Children's Magazine', December 1911. A large wooden stick is being used to push the wood-wool firmly into the plush body.

THE TEDDY BEAR

Although various kinds of plush bear have featured amongst the many different soft toy animals produced in the past, none have remained so popular as the teddy bear. Prior to the invention of the teddy, bears were usually represented on all fours and were known in the nursery as 'Bruins', just as rabbits are often called bunnies by young children.

The true origin of the teddy bear is uncertain, but it probably owes its name to the twenty-sixth President of the United States, Theodore or 'Teddy' Roosevelt. He was fond of the outdoor life, particularly bear hunting. While visiting the southern States to settle a boundary dispute between Mississippi and Louisiana, Roosevelt took time off to hunt. After an uneventful day, a bear cub was captured and brought to him. His refusal to shoot the defenceless animal became the subject of a political cartoon by Clifford K. Berryman, which

appeared in the *Washington Post* on 16th November 1902. Subsequently, an enterprising New York shopkeeper, Morris Michtom, spotted the cartoon and made a stuffed plush bear toy for sale in his novelty store. It sat in the window alongside a copy of Berryman's drawing and a label, 'Teddy's Bear'. It is said that the Russian-born Mr Michtom wrote to the President asking for permission to use his name in connection with the toy, and Roosevelt is reported to have replied that he would be surprised if his association should have any effect on its sales. He was to be proved wrong, for the bear was an instant success and Michtom soon gave up his shop to found the Ideal Toy and Novelty Company, which became one of the largest and most successful toy businesses in the United States. The original model for the first Teddy's Bear now resides in the Smithsonian Institution in Washington DC.

Advertisement for Gross and Schild's 'Bruno the Talking Bear', from 'Games and Toys, 1925.

Despite the Ideal Toy Company's claim to be the originator of the teddy bear, some believe that Germany is its true native land. Certainly the majority of early teddy bears were made in Germany and imported to both Europe and the United States. Of these, many originated from the Steiff firm and some assert that it was Margarete Steiff's nephew who was directly responsible for introducing the teddy bear to the market. Richard Steiff joined the family business in 1897 following an art school training. In about 1902, it is said that he gave his aunt designs for a stuffed plush bear based on drawings he had made of bear cubs in Stuttgart Zoo. The toy, known as 'Friend Petz', was subsequently made up and added to the range of stuffed animals sent to the Leipzig Toy Fair in 1903. Later, Steiff's American agent ordered three thousand because of the current rage for bears in the United States, and from that moment the small family business expanded dramatically in order to keep up with the demand for teddy bears. The period 1903-7, for example, is known by the Steiff company as the *Bährenjahre* (Bear Years), when the production of teddy bears outweighed all other soft toys. The number of bears produced by the firm rose from some 12,000 in 1903 to a staggering 974,000 per year by 1907.

Teddy bears were certainly established toys by about 1906 for at about this time they were appearing in toy trade catalogues as 'teddy bears' rather than 'Teddy's Bear' or just plush bears. It was thought, however, that the craze for these toys might pass, especially following Roosevelt's failure to gain a third term of office in 1909. In the same year an Atlanta firm created a possum soft toy in an attempt to rival the teddy bear after the President elect William Taft had eaten their local delicacy of roast possum and had sung its praises. Needless to say, the possum toy was short-lived and the teddy bear remained a best seller.

The early teddy bear's body consisted of an elongated bag of Yorkshire Cloth stuffed with wood-wool, featuring a prominent humped back. Its swivel head had a long muzzle with boot-button eyes, whilst its long limbs possessed feet like a doll. Its nose, mouth and claws were embroidered with black or brown thread and its pads were generally of felt or leather. Growlers (that is, internal mechanisms for making the bears 'growl' when the toy was tipped back and forth) were inserted into the teddy bear's body from an early date. Sadly, many of these no longer work although their hard pre-

Above left: *Very rare 'Peter' bear, about 1925, produced by Gebrüder Süssenguth of Neustadt, near Coburg, Germany. When the head is turned, the 'googlie' glass eyes and bisque tongue move from side to side.*
Above right: *Unusual teddy bear whose tail operates the swivelling action of the head, so revealing either a happy or a sad face; 4⅜ inches (110 mm) long.*

Right: *Child's muff in the shape of a teddy bear, to be hung around the neck. The hands are kept warm in the bear's fat plush body.*

13

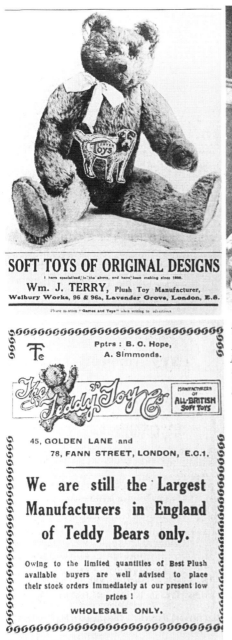

SOFT TOYS OF ORIGINAL DESIGNS

I have specialised in the above, and have been making since 1890.

Wm. J. TERRY, Plush Toy Manufacturer,
Welbury Works, 96 & 96a, Lavender Grove, London, E.8.

Please mention "Games and Toys" when writing to advertisers.

𝕋ₑ

Pptrs : B. C. Hope,
A. Simmonds.

MANUFACTURERS OF
ALL-BRITISH
SOFT TOYS

45, GOLDEN LANE and
78, FANN STREET, LONDON, E.C.1.

We are still the Largest Manufacturers in England of Teddy Bears only.

Owing to the limited quantities of Best Plush available buyers are well advised to place their stock orders immediately at our present low prices !

WHOLESALE ONLY.

Above left: *Advertisement for William J. Terry's teddy bears in 'Games and Toys', 1919. Unfortunately, no teddy bears from this firm have as yet been positively identified.*

Above right: *A stall of teddy bears belonging to W. H. Jones, a pioneer of the British soft toy industry, at a toy fair in 1915.*

Advertisement for the Teddy Toy Company of 1918. The toys are known to have worn card swing tags bearing their trademark 'TTC' or 'SOFTANLITE' but these have generally been mislaid over the years.

Three 'Schuco' teddy bears made in about 1935 by the German firm Schreyer and Company (1912-78). Their tails act as levers for moving their heads from side to side. In the Bethnal Green Museum of Childhood.

sence can be felt within some of the early bears' chests.

As the teddy bear grew in popularity, many manufacturers tried to introduce novelty elements into what was, generally speaking, a uniform product. For example, as early as 1907, the Strauss Manufacturing Company of New York was offering an amazing 'Self Whistling Bear'. Several teddy bears with sparkling eyes were available, including that produced by Gustav Forster of Neustadt in 1926, the battery for illuminating the green eyes being hidden in a knapsack on the bear's back. Some teddy bears in the 1930s were produced with moving tails, which acted as levers for moving the head, examples being the German 'Schuco' bears and the Chiltern 'Wagmee' series made by H. G. Stone in England.

Teddy bears were predominantly German in origin before the First World War. In Britain, they were produced by some of the early soft toy manufacturers, including W. J. Terry, the Teddy Toy Company and J. K. Farnell. The latter made an 'Alpha' bear exclusively for Harrods. This may well have been the original 'Winnie the Pooh', for it was from this store that a bear was purchased for Christopher Robin Milne's first birthday in 1921; it later became the central character in A. A. Milne's famous stories and is now on display at the New York Public Library.

The new English soft toy firms of the 1920s and 1930s all made a range of teddy bears. In this period, the teddy bear was beginning to change in shape and materials. The back hump disappeared and the muzzle was shortened, while English bears of this date were made with shorter arms. Glass eyes replaced the traditional black boot buttons, and a kind of American cloth ('rexine') or sometimes velveteen was used in place of felt for the pads. Kapok stuffing was more frequently preferred. Bears also began to be made of rayon plush in various colours, and later plastic eyes and noses were added. Identification is difficult without the secure

15

"Producers of Beautiful Models"

Above left: *Advertisement for the 'Ally-Bears' produced by Harwin and Company during the First World War. From the start of the teddy bear craze many were produced in clothes as popular mascots for both children and adults alike.*
Above right: *1930s advertisement for 'Alpha' teddy bears made by J. K. Farnell. Such a bear may have been the original 'Winnie the Pooh'.*

A large teddy bear made in England in about 1927. Its wide head and short arms are typical of English bears of this period. In the Bethnal Green Museum of Childhood.

16

Two Merrythought teddy bears. The clothed 1930s bear has a typical woven pre-Second World War tag: 'MERRYTHOUGHT HYGIENIC TOYS. MADE IN ENGLAND.' 'Merrythought' is an old English word for wishbone, hence the design of the swing tag of the 1970s bear. In the Bethnal Green Museum of Childhood.

Three teddy bears of the 1930s and 1940s made by Chad Valley. Like many English soft toys of the period, they are stuffed with kapok. In the Bethnal Green Museum of Childhood.

presence of a maker's label. Teddy bears made of sheepskin usually date from the Second World War when the production of Yorkshire Cloth ceased.

The post-war years saw the introduction of man-made materials for the manufacture of teddy bears. Many lost their jointed doll-like shape until the renaiss-' ance in the late 1970s and 1980s, when manufacturers once again began producing the traditionally styled teddy bear to meet the demands of modern 'arctophiles'.

Left: *A teddy bear of about 1960, made by Wendy Boston Playsafe Toys, who first introduced the 'safe eye' and completely washable soft toy in the 1950s.*

Below: *Rare surviving label from a cardboard box originally containing an 'Omega' teddy bear made in the mid 1930s by the British United Toy Manufacturing Company.*

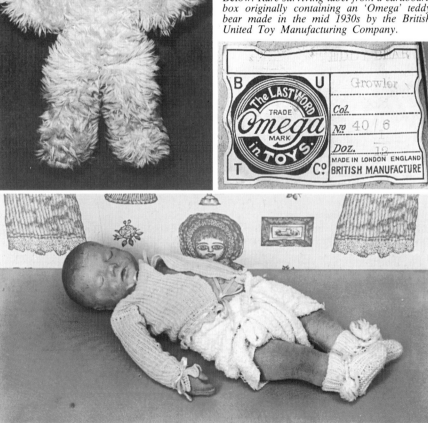

Käthe Kruse's 'Traumerchen' (Little Dreamer) stockinette infant doll, first made in 1925. Strategically placed bags of sand give it a lifelike weight, while the applied spiral of stockinette belly-button adds further realism.

18

Left: *Oil-painted cloth doll with moulded face by Martha Chase of Pawtucket, Rhode Island, USA. The thickly painted hair is typical, as opposed to the earlier and less realistic Izannah Walker dolls.*

Right: *Steiff felt-faced doll of about 1920, representing an Argentinian cowboy. In the Bethnal Green Museum of Childhood.*

CLOTH DOLLS

Like other soft toys, simple rag dolls must have been made in the home ever since the invention of weaving. However, as far as we know, their commercial manufacture dates from the mid nineteenth century. The famous wax-doll makers, the Montanari family, for example, in about 1855, produced a range called 'English Rag Babies', with cloth faces drawn over a wax mask. Moulded mask-like faces of painted cloth could also be bought for use with home-made rag dolls in the 1870s. Sadly, none are known to survive.

Like printed cut-out toys, many of the earliest known commercially made rag dolls still in existence were those produced in America. Here, dolls of fabric were produced to rival the imported European examples, whose fragility

would not have been suitable for the tough frontier life.

The earliest known maker of this genre was Mrs Izannah Walker of Central Falls, Rhode Island. Her method was patented in 1873 and involved pressing stockinette, backed with stuffing and glue-stiffened cloth, into a mould to form the face. The back of the head was made in the same way and the two halves were stitched together and stuffed. The features, including the hair, were delineated with oil paints, while the body was made of cream-coloured sateen.

Similar in style are the sized and painted stockinette-faced dolls made by Martha Chase of nearby Pawtucket, which date from 1889 to about 1935. The Chase Stockinette Doll Company produced many different sizes and models of

Left: *Old Peasant Woman doll, about 1913, made by Steiff, with a cloth body, felt face and lower arms. Reproductions are now being made by the firm. In the Bethnal Green Museum of Childhood.*
Right: *This plump, side-glancing, fashionably dressed boy is a typical example of the Italian 'Lenci' range of child dolls. 'Lenci' dolls are marked on the foot or with a button on the body.*

cloth doll. The most interesting and long-surviving, however, were probably the range of waterproof dolls which Mrs Chase was asked to produce from 1910 for use in a hospital training school. Made of oilcloth and waterproof paint, they even came equipped with an all-rubber internal system.

Several other painted cloth dolls were produced in the United States, such as the 'Columbian' dolls of Emma and Marietta Smith, or the 'Philadelphian Baby' patented in 1900 by the J. B. Sheppard Company. They are more readily found in American collections although Chase and Walker dolls occasionally come up for auction in Britain.

In Europe the dolls most comparable in style to the American type of moulded cloth doll are those of Berlin dollmaker Käthe Kruse (1883-1968). Her dolls, however, are far more sophisticated and lifelike in conception and are highly collectable world-wide. Mrs Kruse began making dolls for her children from towels and sand, with a potato head. She spent four years perfecting these home-made dolls with help from her sculptor husband until 1911, when the first Käthe Kruse doll was patented. The heads were made of flesh-coloured nettle-cloth over a wax mask and reinforced with glue-stiffened gauze, pressed into a bronze mould. They were stuffed with wood-wool and deer hair. Later, in the early 1920s, an elastic tricot material was used on the body and head. All the faces were hand-painted until 1952, when coloured plastic faces were introduced. Käthe Kruse dolls with human hair wigs date from 1929. Before this, hair was simply painted on to the dolls. The dolls are usually stamped with 'Kruse' and have a number on the foot. Many different types of doll were produced in a variety of costumes, including shop window mannikins, now very collectable. Best known are the stockinette infant dolls or 'Sand Babies', which contained bags of sand, so giving the doll a lifelike weight. They were often used in child-care training.

In Britain commercially made rag dolls of stockinette and muslin were made during the First World War when all German goods were banned. For example, there were those designed by Mrs Elizabeth Houghton for the Isle of Wight's Shanklin Toy Industry, as well as the chubby muslin babes produced in Sylvia Pankhurst's East London Federation Toy Factory in Bow. Dean's Rag Book Company also produced a new series of quaint cuddly dolls with woolly hair called 'Moppietopp' in 1914.

Felt dolls have their origins in Germany where they were made principally by Margarete Steiff from 1894. These fully jointed figures of, for example, soldiers, sailors, musicians, circus types and children, all with a centre facial seam and a 'button in the ear', are similar to the 'Dot's Dolls' designed by Miss Dorothy Harwin for the London firm of Harwin and Company from 1914.

From the 1920s, a more realistic felt doll, without the face seam, was produced by several companies in Europe. This was achieved by hot-pressing stiffened felt, usually with a buckram backing, over a metal mould. Many dolls were produced in this manner and it is sometimes difficult to determine their maker if the trademarks have been removed. Some of the most beautiful examples of this type were made in Italy by Enrico and Elena Scavini of Turin, whose trademark was Madame Scavini's pet-name: 'Lenci'. 'Lenci' dolls were made from about 1920 onwards, generally of felt with mohair wigs and painted features. The most typical designs were the plump children with sideways glances and pouting mouths, always stylishly dressed in felt, organdie or sometimes fashionable knitwear. Red Indian and Japanese dolls, as well as other figures in regional costume, were also made.

In Britain, a number of firms produced moulded felt dolls from the early 1920s as cheaper alternatives to the expensive 'Lenci' range. Chad Valley and Dean's Rag Book Company were the first to make a variety of felt dolls. Norah Wellings, originally a designer with Chad Valley, produced mainly felt and velvet dolls and some plush soft toy animals from 1926 to 1960. She was particularly well known for her 'Jolliboy' sailor dolls in blue velvet uniforms, which were sold as mascots on cruise ships; for South Sea Islanders of brown velvet with raffia 'grass' skirts; as well as for a 'Harry the Hawk' felt doll with a parachute, made during the Second World War with sale proceeds going to Royal Air Force Comforts.

Farnell manufactured felt dolls under the tradenames 'Alpha Cherub' and 'Joy-Day' from 1935 and they also produced portrait dolls of moulded felt representing Edward VIII and George VI.

Two felt portrait dolls representing Edward VIII in Highland dress and in plus-fours, made by J. K. Farnell in about 1937. Upon the king's abdication, the moulds were adapted to produce similar dolls of George VI.

Left: *Princess Elizabeth doll with pressed felt face, fixed glass eyes, mohair wig and velvet limbs. Made by Chad Valley as part of their 'Bambina' range in the late 1920s.*

Centre: *Chad Valley felt doll, 1937, with painted features, dressed in an attractive emerald green felt suit. The firm's woven label is stitched to the sole of one foot; 18 inches (458 mm) high.*

Right: *Life-sized felt-faced doll, with cotton body, made by Dean's Rag Book Company as part of their 'Playmate Series' of 1938; 43¼ inches (110 cm) high. In the Bethnal Green Museum of Childhood.*

Merrythought manufactured a few felt dolls during the 1930s. The majority of these British dolls had painted features although some, like Chad Valley's 'Bambina' series and Norah Wellings's 'Cora' dolls of the late 1920s, had fixed glass eyes. Interesting examples to look out for include the four royal dolls produced by Chad Valley in 1938, representing the Princesses Elizabeth and Margaret Rose and their cousins, Princess Alexandra and Prince Edward.

Dean's Rag Book Company made several dolls for advertising purposes, including 'Miss Betty Oxo', available originally through saving Oxo stock cube tokens. An example of this moulded felt doll in her fur-trimmed purple coat, hat and muff can be seen at the Museum of Childhood, Edinburgh. The production of felt art dolls generally ceased during the 1950s, although both Steiff and Lenci are presently reproducing some of their old designs.

During the 1920s and 1930s some of the companies mentioned also made long-legged dolls known as 'boudoir' or 'sofa' dolls, originally intended as mascots for young ladies. Many doubled as nightdress cases, with wide skirts for this purpose, such as Norah Wellings's gypsy doll at Pollock's Toy Museum, London. Some of these boudoir dolls originated in France and were elegantly dressed in silks and velvets to represent flappers, pierrots or film stars, their faces often constructed from stockinette stretched over moulded card.

22

Popular postcard of 1906 based on the illustrations of Florence K. Upton in her 'Golliwogg' books. Early manufactured gollies were made with noses like the original character.

THE GOLLIWOG AND OTHER CHARACTER SOFT TOYS

Since the early days of commercially made soft toys, manufacturers have looked to a variety of sources for inspiration, including children's books, newspaper comic strips, the cinema and, in the post-war period, the television. Another classic of the nursery, the golliwog, belongs to this type of soft toy.

The golliwog, or golly, first became popular in England at the end of the nineteenth century and was based on a character from a series of thirteen books describing the adventures of 'Golliwogg' (sic) and five wooden Dutch dolls, published between 1895 and 1908. They were illustrated by Florence K. Upton (1873-1922), with verses by her mother, Bertha. Miss Upton based the character on a black rag doll she had played with as a child in America. This doll, the wooden dolls, the manuscripts and the original watercolour illustrations, were given to the Red Cross in 1917 and auctioned by Christie's in order to buy an ambulance

to aid the war effort. The toys were later presented to Chequers, the Prime Minister's country residence in Buckinghamshire, where they were displayed until given on long loan to the Bethnal Green Museum of Childhood.

One cannot discuss the golliwog's popularity without also mentioning the jam manufacturers James Robertson and Sons, who adopted this character as their mascot in 1910. A few years previously, one of the sons had visited the United States and had come across children playing with black rag dolls which they called 'gollies' (presumably derived from 'dolly') and which resembled that belonging to Florence Upton. The now famous 'golly' symbol used on Robertson's jam has probably done more to popularise the toy than the original books, which are now out of print.

Like their American predecessors, many gollies have been made at home. *The Best Way Book of 1200 Household*

23

Left: *Golliwog of kapok-stuffed velveteen, made by J. K. Farnell. Woven label on foot:* 'FARNELL'S ALPHA TOYS. MADE IN ENGLAND.' *'Alpha' was registered as a trademark on 17th November 1925. In the Bethnal Green Museum of Childhood.*

Right: *'Struwwelpeter' ('Shock-headed Peter'), a character from Dr Heinrich Hoffmann's 'Cautionary Tales' of 1845, was produced in felt by Steiff from 1911 to 1927.   In the Museum of Childhood, Edinburgh.*

Hints & Recipes, dating from the 1914-18 war, gives instructions on making a home-made 'gollywog' from shiny sateen and darning wool. By about 1910, several companies were producing their own versions. Early golliwogs have a more realistic profile like the Upton illustrations, such as those produced by Steiff and the Star Manufacturing Company in about 1913. Later gollies are generally flat-faced, either for ease and economy, or perhaps in imitation of the Robertson's mascot. Before the First World War, Dean's Rag Book Company was making printed cloth sheets of golliwogs to be made up at home. Coloured velvets were often used in both handmade and commercially produced dolls, particularly in the 1920s and 1930s, in examples such as the 'Rigmel Gollywog' of 1937, dressed in a green velveteen suit with

white stripes, made by the Staffordshire firm of Richard Sons and Allwin Limited. Cotton material has also been used in their manufacture. An unusual example of a golliwog was Dean's 'Mr Smith', a white version, produced in 1966.

The golliwog was the earliest of various soft toys based on children's book characters. In the early days of the company, Dean's produced some printed sheets of popular nursery figures, including those found in Lewis Carroll's *Alice in Wonderland*. Steiff also made characters from German children's stories, such as 'Struwwelpeter', and the mischievous pair 'Max and Moritz'.

Several new children's books involving animals, now classics, were published in the 1920s and 1930s and supplied ideas for soft toys. For example, A. A. Milne's *Winnie the Pooh* was first published

24

in 1926. By the 1930s, both the Teddy Toy Company and Chad Valley were producing Christopher Robin dolls and 'Pooh' bears, as well as their famous companions. At the same time, the Teddy Toy Company was also making soft toys based on Hugh Lofting's 'Dr Doolittle' books, which had reached British children in 1922. The 1930s saw Farnell producing two famous literary elephants, Jean de Brunhoff's 'Babar' and Katharine Tozer's 'Mumfie'. Peter Pan' was also immortalised in felt and velvet by both Farnell and Dean's Rag Book Company (who also made a 'Wendy' doll) at this time, with royalties going to the Great Ormond Street Hospital for Sick Children, London.

Both popular film stars, such as Charlie Chaplin, Shirley Temple and Marlene Dietrich, and animated cartoon characters inspired soft toys in the 1920s and 1930s. 'Felix the Cat' became known to the British public at about this time through Pathe's *Eve and Everybody's Film Review* at the cinema. Originally created in about 1920 by the American animator Pat Sullivan, he was frequently reproduced as a toy, on children's china and in printed material. In Britain, Felix soft toys date from 1924, when several companies, including Dean's Rag Book Company, J. K. Farnell and the Teddy Toy Company, created their own plush or printed cloth versions of the cat 'who kept on walking'. However, his popularity was outstripped, a few years later, by that of Walt Disney's greatest creation, Mickey Mouse. He first appeared in 1928 in a silent film, *Plane Crazy*, as well as in the better known *Steamboat Willie*. The following year, Dean's produced their Mickey Mouse mascot doll in eight sizes and Mickey's girlfriend, Minnie, was soon added to the range, along with Donald Duck and Pluto the Dog. 'Popeye, the Sailor Man', who gained enormous strength through eating spinach, came to the screen in 1933 after much success in comic strips. Two years later Dean's had come up with a Popeye rag doll in soft stuffed velvet. Walt Disney's *Snow White* was seen at the cinema from 1937 and, in turn, Chad Valley produced dolls of 'Snow White and the Seven Dwarfs' in kapok-stuffed felt. Merrythought produced a similar set in the mid 1950s.

Left: Katharine Tozer's 'Mumfie', produced by J. K. Farnell in 1937, made of white velvet and cerise felt. It was 10 inches (254 mm) high and originally sold for 5s 11d.

Right: Two Mickey Mouse 'Evripose' mascots produced by Dean's Rag Book Company in eight sizes in about 1930. There is an internal wire armature inside each felt and velveteen body. 'REGD NO 750611' printed on chin; 6 inches (153 mm) and 8 inches (203 mm) high. In the Bethnal Green Museum of Childhood.

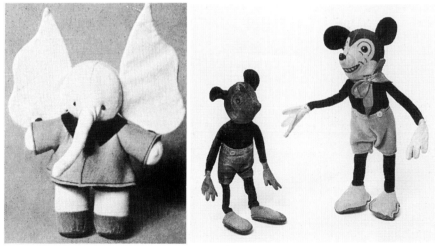

The 'Daily Mirror' pets of the 1930s, Pip, Squeak and Wilfred. In the Bethnal Green Museum of Childhood.

'Bonzo the Dog' was another important figure in the soft toy world at this time. This comical bull terrier pup, first created in 1912 by George E. Studdy (1878-1948), featured in the *Daily Sketch* as well as appearing in a series of silent cartoon films in 1924. Chad Valley were making soft toy versions of Bonzo, in nine sizes and in various positions, from 1929. However, these should not be confused with Merrythought's Bonzo of the mid 1950s made of pink velveteen.

Cartoon characters made famous through newspapers and other sources inspired several toys, and none more so than the *Daily Mirror* pets 'Pip, Squeak and Wilfred': respectively, a dog, a penguin and a baby rabbit (who could only say 'gug' and 'nunc' for uncle). The comic strip ran from 1919 until 1953, and in 1921 several firms began producing the three animals. Wilfred was particularly popular as a soft toy, being the mascot of the fan club 'The Wilfredian League of Gugnuncs' formed in 1927.

Other newspaper personalities which are now almost forgotten were produced in soft toy form. These include the *Daily Mirror*'s 'Nero the Newshound', made by Dean's in 1935, while in the same year Merrythought produced 'The Nipper', a rag doll representing Brian White's mischievous toddler, who appeared in the *Daily Mail* from 1933 to 1947.

Popular songs of the day also inspired Dean's Rag Book Company to make several soft toys, including 'Dickie Blob', a black velvet toy (1927), 'Tiddlywinks', a plush dog (1935), and 'Lupino Lane', a cloth doll representing the singer of the popular 'Lambeth Walk' of 1938.

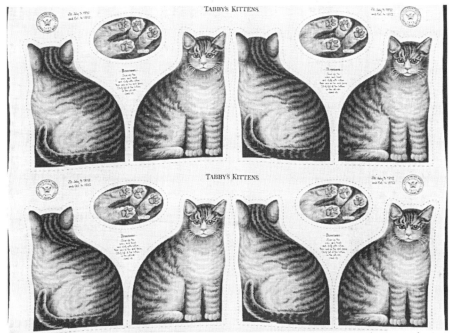

'Tabby's Kittens' (1892) by the Arnold Print Works, then one of the largest manufacturers of prints and dress goods in the United States. They could be purchased by the yard at drapers' shops.

PRINTED CLOTH CUT-OUT TOYS

The commercially produced printed cut-out toy differs little from that produced in the home. Manufacture involved printing the front and back outlines of a toy on to a roll of cotton fabric, together with instructions for assembly. The toys were cut out, sewn together and stuffed. For the latter process, Dean's Rag Book Company recommended 'fine wood wool or granulated cork . . . obtained from glass and china stores for a few pence'. In the United States, cotton batting, sawdust or bran were recommended fillings.

Following the development of cheaper textile printing, these rag toys were manufactured by several American cotton fabric firms from the 1880s. A Santa Claus by Edward S. Peck of Brooklyn was the first to be patented, on 20th December 1886. A few examples of this appealing two-piece muslin doll, designed by Thomas Nast, still exist today. Another early example is the 'Christmas Stocking' patented by S. W. Howe of

New York in 1889. Over 2 feet (61 cm) long, it carried the verse 'Hang up the Baby's Stocking. Be sure you don't forget. The little dimpled darling, Has ne'er seen Xmas yet.'

The majority of early American printed cut-out toys date from the 1890s. The two most prolific firms producing them were the Arnold Print Works of North Adams, Massachusetts, and the Art Fabric Mills of New York. The Arnold Print Works produced the famous 'Palmer Cox Brownies' (patented on 15th January 1892). Examples of these twelve comical bow-legged figures can be seen at the Museums of Childhood in Edinburgh and Anglesey. This company also produced several other printed toys in the same year. The dolls included a charming 'Piccaninny', 'Little Red Riding Hood' and 'Pitti Sing', a Japanese girl in a kimono. The Arnold Print Works also produced several animals including 'Tabby Cat', 'Bow Wow' (the pug puppy)

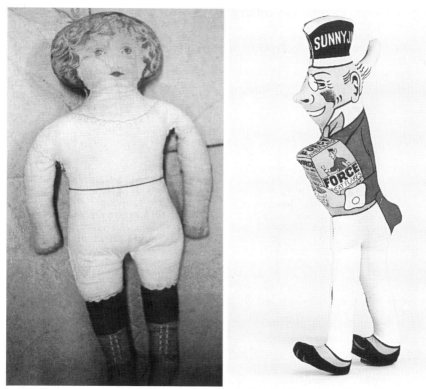

Left: *'Life Size Doll' of heavy sateen made by the Art Fabric Mills of New York. The patent date, '13th Feb. 1900', is printed on the sole of one foot.*

Right: *'Sunny Jim', the printed cloth advertising doll for Force Wheatflakes. Designed by Minnie Maude Hanff in the United States in 1902, it was available by post either ready made up or in sheet form; 16 inches (406 mm) high.*

and a hen, complete with her four chicks. Many of the toys possessed an additional oval base, printed with pads, claws or feet, into which cardboard could be inserted to give the toy greater stability. Other refinements in this style of toy could also be seen in the jointed cloth doll produced by the company in 1893; this had darts in all the usual jointed parts of the figure, enabling her to sit down. She left the factory wearing only printed underclothes, boots and a string of beads so that the child could dress her using clothes from another doll's wardrobe.

The Art Fabric Mills' most famous printed cloth toy was their 'Life Size Doll made so that Babies clothes will now fit Dollie', which was first produced in 1900.

Life-size dolls were made by several firms such as the Elms and Sellon Company's 'Standish No-Brake Life Size Doll' patented in 1910 by Edward Gibson. At about the same time, Butterick, the maker of dress patterns, produced the 'Butterick Rag Doll' 'to teach the future mother to dress the future child'.

Printed dolls and toys became popular, particularly in the United States, as advertising gimmicks, sometimes known as 'premiums'. They could be obtained by sending box tops and a coin to the product manufacturer. It may be difficult to identify the product promoted by such dolls, as brand names would have been printed on the area of wastage. Examples of this type are 'Aunt Jemima and her

Rag Doll Family' (about 1910), which could be obtained by collecting the coupons of Aunt Jemima's Pancake Flour. Their names only (Uncle Mose, Wade Davis, Diana Jemima as well as Aunt Jemima) are printed on the fronts or backs of the dolls. Others, however, are easier to identify. The 'Cerota Doll' of the same period, a farmer's boy in red breeches and braces, has 'Cerota Flour' printed boldly across his shirt. The Kellogg Company's 'Goldilocks and the Three Bears', produced in 1925, all display their maker's trademark, while the 'Quaker Crackels Doll' of 1930 carries a box of Quaker Oats in his back pocket. Still produced today is the 'Sunny Jim' doll, which began advertising Force Wheatflakes from about 1915 in the United States and from the 1920s in Britain. Not only food manufacturers offered premiums. In 1933, Fels and Company produced 'Anty Drudge', a bespectacled old woman wearing a dress overprinted with the words 'Fels Naptha Soap' and holding a bar of this product.

In Britain, the printed rag toy industry was dominated by Dean's Rag Book Company, one of the earliest soft toy manufacturers in existence. Originally part of the well established publishers Dean and Son, the Rag Book Company was formed in 1903 by Henry Samuel Dean in a factory behind Fleet Street. The first rag book of unbleached calico, hand-printed in one colour only, the founder's own invention, was a book for children 'who wear their food and eat their clothes'.

It has been said that Dean's first rag dolls were produced in book form but none are known to have survived. A fire in their new Elephant and Castle premises in 1916 destroyed many valuable early products and archives. The earliest surviving Dean's catalogue dates from 1912-13. Here, their 'Knockabout Toy Sheets', originally costing from 6d to 1s 6d, are described. These included a 'Life Size Baby Doll', 'Mr Puck' (from *A Midsummer Night's Dream)*, 'Humpty Dumpty', 'Red Riding Hood' and 'Cin-

'Master Puck', made by Dean's Rag Book Company in about 1911, and their 'Knockabout Land' rag book describing some of their 'Knockabout Toys' in production at the time.

derella'. There were also several animal toys in 'soft woolly cloth', such as three teddy bears ('Mamma Bear, Teddy and Sissy'), three lucky black cats and a life-size dog and cat. Dean's also produced a smaller 'threepenny' range, which were particularly suitable for 'kindergarten sewing classes'. Some of the larger printed dolls and animals were sold by the firm as ready-made toys.

There were a few other companies producing printed rag toys in Britain at this time, including the London firms of Henry J. Hughes, Samuel Finsbury and Company and Bell and Francis. During the First World War, toy soldiers and nurses were particularly popular. The printed cloth toy is still enjoyed today owing to its relative cheapness and simplicity. Collectors should be wary of contemporary reproductions of early examples.

Left: *A printed fabric Gnome of 1910-14 (by Dean's), filled with granulated cork. The maker's famous trademark of two dogs, designed by Stanley Berkley, can be found beneath the left foot. In the Bethnal Green Museum of Childhood.*

Below: *'Teddie and Peggie' from Dean's 'Weiderseim' series of 1912/13 (after their designer, Grace Weiderseim). By 1920 they were referred to as the 'Goo Goo' series.*

FURTHER READING

Axe, John. *The Magic of Merrythought.* Hobby House Press, 1986. Detailed catalogue of Merrythought's soft toys.

Brooks, Jacki. *The Complete Encyclopedia of Teddy Bears.* Australian Doll Digest, 1990.

Bull, Peter. *The Teddy Bear Book.* House of Nisbet, 1983. By one of the pioneers of 'arctophily'. (First issued as *Bear With Me*, Hutchinson, 1969.)

Cieslik, Jürgen and Marianne. *Button in Ear.* Verlag Marianne Cieslik, 1989.

Cieslik, Jürgen and Marianne. *Steiff Teddy Bears.* Verlag Marianne Cieslik, 1995.

Cockrill, Pauline. *The Teddy Bear Encyclopedia.* Dorling Kindersley, 1993.

Cockrill, Pauline. *The Ultimate Teddy Bear Book.* Dorling Kindersley, 1991.

Coleman, Dorothy S. *Lenci Dolls: Fabulous Figures of Felt.* Hobby House Press, 1977. Highly detailed survey.

Conway, Shirley, and Wilson, Jean. *100 Years of Steiff: 1880-1980.* Hobby House Press, 1983.

Hutchings, Margaret. *Teddy Bears and How to Make Them.* Mills & Boon, 1964, 1977.

King, Constance Eileen. *The Collector's History of Dolls.* St Martin's Press, 1978. Chapter on cloth dolls.

King, Constance Eileen. *The Encyclopaedia of Toys.* Robert Hale, 1978. Section on teddy bears and soft toys.

King, Constance Eileen. *Antique Toys and Dolls.* Studio Vista/Christies, 1979. Chapter on soft toys.

Mansell, Colette. *The Collector's Guide to British Dolls since 1920.* Robert Hale, 1983. Includes useful guide to dating 'Sunny Jim' dolls.

Mullins, Linda. *Teddy Bears Past and Present.* Hobby House Press, Volume I 1986, Volume II 1991. Covers all the main manufacturers as well as a section on golliwogs.

Mullins, Linda. *American Teddy Bear Encyclopedia.* Hobby House Press, 1995.

Pearson, Sue. *Bears.* De Agostini Editions, 1995.

Picot, Geneviève and Gérard. *Teddy Bears.* Weidenfeld & Nicolson, 1988.

Richter, Lydia. *Treasury of Käthe Kruse Dolls.* HP Books, 1984.

Schoonmaker, Patricia N. *A Collector's History of the Teddy Bear.* Hobby House Press, 1981.

Walker, Frances, and Whitton, Margaret. *Playthings by the Yard: The Story of Cloth Dolls.* Hadley Printing Company, 1973. Survey of American printed cut-out toys.

Waring, Philippa and Peter. *The Teddy Bear Lover's Book.* Souvenir Press, 1985.

PERIODICALS

The UK Teddy Bear Guide is published annually by Hugglets, PO Box 290, Brighton, East Sussex BN2 1DR, who also publish quarterly the *Hugglets' Teddy Bear Magazine* and run the British Teddy Bear Association. *The Teddy Bear and Friends* is the soft toy collectors' magazine published six times a year by Hobby House Press, 900 Frederick Street, Cumberland MD 21502, USA. *Teddy Bear Times* is published bi-monthly by Ashdown Publishing, Avalon Court, Star Road, Partridge Green, West Sussex RH13 8RY. *Teddy Bear Scene* is published bi-monthly by EMF Publishing (SM Magazine Distribution Ltd, 6 Leigham Court Road, Streatham, London SW6 2PG). *Teddy Bear Review* is also published bi-monthly by Collector Communications Corp, 170 Fifth Avenue, NY 10010, USA. *Bear Facts Review* is published by the Australian Doll Digest, PO Box 503, Moss Vale, NSW 2577, Australia. There are many useful articles on the soft toy industry in *Games and Toys*, the journal of the British toy trade published from 1914 to 1979.

PLACES TO VISIT

Visitors are advised to find out dates and times of opening before making a special journey.

GREAT BRITAIN

Arundel Toy and Military Museum, 23 High Street, Arundel, West Sussex BN18 9AD. Telephone: 01903 883101.

The Bear Museum, 38 Dragon Street, Petersfield, Hampshire GU31 4JJ. Telephone: 01730 265108. Bears for sale in the shop and bear repairs.

Bethnal Green Museum of Childhood, Cambridge Heath Road, London E2 9PA. Telephone: 0181-983 5200.

Broadway Bears and Dolls, 76 High Street, Broadway, Worcestershire WR12 7AJ. Telephone: 01386 858323.

Dewsbury Museum, Crow Nest Park, Heckmondwike Road, Dewsbury, West Yorkshire WF13 2SA. Telephone: 01924 468171.

Judges' Lodgings, Church Street, Lancaster, Lancashire LA1 1YS. Telephone: 01524 32808.

London Toy and Model Museum, 21-23 Craven Hill, London W2 3EN. Telephone: 0171-706 8000. Peter Bull's Bequest and Paddington Bear archive.

Museum of Childhood, 42 High Street, Edinburgh EH1 1TG. Telephone: 0131-529 4142.

Museum of Childhood, Sudbury Hall, Sudbury, Derbyshire DE6 5HT. Telephone: 01283 585305.

Museum of Childhood and Bears and Friends, 41 Meeting House Lane, Brighton BN1 1HB. Telephone: 01273 208940.

Museum of Childhood Memories, 1 Castle Street, Beaumaris, Anglesey, Gwynedd LL58 8AP. Telephone: 01248 712498.

Pollock's Toy Museum, 1 Scala Street, London W1P 1LT. Telephone: 0171-636 3452.

Scotland's Teddy Bear Museum, The Wynd, Melrose, Scotland TD6 9LB. Telephone: 0189682 2464.

Teddy Bear Museum, 19 Greenhill Street, Stratford-upon-Avon, Warwickshire CV37 6LF. Telephone: 01789 293160. Hundreds of teddy bears from more than twenty countries in a variety of settings.

Teddy Bears of Witney, 99 High Street, Witney, Oxfordshire OX8 6LY. Telephone: 01993 702616. Shop and museum. Famous bears on display including Alfonzo, Theodore and Aloyius and many of the original bears in *The Teddy Bear Encyclopedia*.

Teddy Bear Shop and Museum, Dale End, Ironbridge, Telford, Shropshire TF8 7NJ. Telephone: 01952 433029. Small collection of original Merrythought soft toys and teddy bears in shop. Run in conjunction with Ironbridge Gorge Museum Trust.

Toy and Teddy Bear Museum and Shop, 373 Clifton Drive North, St Annes, Lancashire FY8 2PA. Telephone: 01253 713705 or 734890.

AUSTRALIA

Romy Roeder's Teddy Bear Shop and Museum, Badgery Avenue, Lawson, NSW 2783.

BELGIUM

Musée du Jouet, 24 Rue de l'Association, 1000 Brussels. Open every day of the year.

GERMANY

The Steiff Museum, Alleenstrasse 2, Postfach 1560, D-7928, Giengen (Brenz). A large collection of original Steiff animals, toys and dolls.

UNITED STATES OF AMERICA

Margaret Woodbury Strong Museum, 1 Manhattan Square, Rochester, New York 14607. Particularly American cloth dolls.

Teddy Bear Museum of Naples, 2511 Pine Ridge Road, Naples, Florida 33942.

ACKNOWLEDGEMENTS

The author is indebted to Anthony Burton and Kevin Edge for reading and commenting on the manuscript; to Pip Barnard and Mike Kitcatt for photographic work; and to Joan Cockrill, Lesley White and Lynnet and Sheila Wilson for the loan of photographs and toys. She is also grateful for the help and advice received from: Halina Pasierbska and other colleagues at Bethnal Green Museum of Childhood; John Heyes and Jill Draper of the Museum of Childhood, Edinburgh; Oliver Holmes of Merrythought Limited; Daphne Scott of Dean's Company (1903) Limited; J. Barber of the Photographic Library, Phillips Fine Art Auctioneers; Bunny Campione of Sothebys; Sylvia Ayling; and Isabel Beattie at the Picture Library, Victoria and Albert Museum.

Illustrations are acknowledged as follows: Pip Barnard, cover, pages 10, 11, 18 (upper right); Trustees of the British Museum, page 4 (top); Archive of Dean's Company (1903) Limited, pages 29, 30 (lower); Museum of Childhood, Edinburgh, pages 4 (lower), 24 (right), 28 (left), all photographed by the author; Phillips Fine Art Auctioneers, pages 1, 13 (upper right), 20 (right); Sothebys, pages 2, 10 (upper right and lower), 13 (upper left and lower), 19 (left), 21, 22 (left), 27; Trustees of the Victoria and Albert Museum, pages 5, 7 (upper right), 8, 9, 15, 16 (lower), 17, 18 (lower), 19 (right), 20 (left), 22 (centre and right), 24 (left), 25 (right), 26, 28 (right), 30 (upper). All the rest are by the author.